Out of My Church Hurt Came Ministry!

By

~ Kennedy Lin~

Out of my Church Hurt Came Ministry

Copyright protected @ Kennedy Lin

ISBN (13-978-1973921783)

This book is based on actual events of my life. Non-disclosure of names is to protect the privacy of others.

DEDICATION

This book is dedicated to some amazing people who have already gone to Glory. These three amazing people saw things in me only they and God could see. Each one played such an incredible part in my life, and I want them to know that all they instilled in me, was not in vain. I am walking in my gifts; I remember my teachings, I remember your humility, I have learned from your Faith in God, your studying of the Word of God, your prayer life and living for the Lord, it is the absolute right thing to do.

To my Grandmother, Girtha Lee Coleman, thank you for teaching me about faith and healing. Thank you so much for being the most amazing example of what godliness looks like.

To my uncles, K.C. Coleman, Sr. teaching me how to pray for hours(lol) and uncle Earl Jean Coleman for teaching me how to study the word of God and instructing me to listen to the Spirit of God. Lastly, Maurice Mantly Price (step father) you taught me I did not necessarily have to be of your DNA to be loved and I cannot thank you enough with my words, hopefully my actions of being the best me and never giving up as you often told me. YOU ROCK!

~Table of Contents~

Acknowledgements

First, I would like to thank My Lord and Savior Jesus Christ for choosing me and trusting me with this assignment and knowing I would do the right thing in honoring Him and revealing what is not of Him. Thank you, hubby(Andreas) for being an amazing life partner and for being strong in areas I am weak, thank you for making my dreams come true as you said you would. Thank you so much to my mother (Peaches) for always believing in me and always telling me "no matter what you do, be the best." I am honestly trying to do my best with all that is set before me. I also would like to thank, my daughter Neek (Bella), who is more than a daughter but my cheerleader, my whole cheering squad, my assistant (non-paid) and the one who never lets me give up. I love you so much. I love you more than you'll ever know. This is what not giving up looks like; WE DID IT in spite of it all, WE DID IT!

Background

I grew up as a Baptist and attended only one church for a large portion of my life. The church, I attended was established by my grandparents and several other families. It was safe to say, I attended church with family (aunts, uncles, and cousins). What I knew of church growing up: reciting Easter speeches (which I disliked), children's choir and the young adult choir (which I disliked as well). I could not sing, nor did I like the hot robes we wore for hours, I did not like the long standing, I was not particularly fond of standing super close to people with hot breath. I was very uncomfortable with people staring at me while we marched and stood in the choir stand, it made me extremely nervous. If only I could fade in the background without ever being noticed that would have been enough for me but that was not and is not my story. Back in the day, you did not have choices or opinions. You just did what you were told, period.

I also attended my uncle tent revivals which were the most intriguing services, to say the least. For the majority of my life, I only attended church with my family. My family was my church family until I moved cross country, and, this is where it gets real. In essence, I was a bit inexperienced when it came to other churches and church people. My grandmother was a devout Christian who did not play when it came to God and living holy. She was the sweetest woman on earth but there was a power she walked in. My grandmother did not play in the natural or the spiritual. I will give an example:

On Sunday mornings, my grandmother would call and speak to my mother, unsure of their conversation in its entirety, but I would hear my mom say something like she was going to drop us off at church but shortly after the conversation, we were all getting ready for church; my mother included. I did not have to be on the other end of the phone to know my grandmother told my mother she had to go to church. But as my grandmother said, you just did (my mother was an adult lol). There was a calmness about my grandmother, but as I mentioned when she spoke you just listened, obeyed and moved with a spirit of urgency.

For my family and I, Sunday's were the days when all the family would get together after church at my grandparents' house, eat, laugh, and sing, my grandmother had a piano in her living room. The best feeling was pulling up and seeing all the cars parked in the cul-de-sac, cousins playing in the street, laughter and conversations coming from the house. Most importantly, the smiles on my grandmother and grandfather's face to see their children and grandchildren all under the same roof. This was the best and it was all I knew.

God blessed me with some amazing people in my family, my grandmother was an incredible, powerful, anointed Woman of God who had the faith to move a million mountains, and to add, I was further blessed with two fabulous uncles who were equally anointed Men of God. All three have gone to be with The Lord but not before imparting in me, what was intended for my journey.

All three played a dynamic role in the Woman of God; I am today. My uncle Earl taught me how to study the word of God and how to allow the Holy Spirit to speak to me and through me. My uncle Earl would get so excited when God revealed scripture to him. I had never seen someone so excited about understanding scripture and obtaining God's knowledge, but him. He would explain to me as you speak the Word of God, let the Holy Spirit speak through you and you would be absolutely amazed at what you begin to know in that very moment. Lastly, my uncle K.C., my uncle K.C. taught me how to pray, when I say this man could pray, he could pray for H O U R S. When he prayed, he prayed with such compassion and power. I never saw anything like it before in my life. Guess, who can pray for hours now(me), he taught me well. When he began teaching me how to pray, I would only say, Jesus wept, due to my intimidation to pray with such a powerful Man of God but nevertheless he continued pushing me to pray. I slid by a few times but then he said, "You have to really pray now". No more baby prayers. He instructed me to let the Spirit of God lead me in what to say. I did just that and, I have been praying ever since. I mean, I really started praying with boldness and authority. He pushed me to pray more and more, and now I am inclined to believe he was on to something, actually I think all three were. Ironically, I, now get questioned of how long am I going to pray, is it going to be a long prayer or short prayer? Anyone who knows me, know that I do not pray short prayers so thank you, uncle K.C.

My grandmother taught me about faith, and I witnessed miracles manifest from her prayers. She would often tell me, "stay on your knees and pray, no matter what your praying about believe God has answered." Who would believe with this amount of faith and power, my grandmother had a third-grade education? But she could read the Word of God and not miss a beat. She was so knowledgeable of the Word. I have so many accounts of her, I could share about the anointing upon her life, I will only name a couple:

When I was in the hospital in the emergency room my grandmother walked in. When "grandma" walked in, any situation you were experiencing was going to be alright. My mother and another young lady were in the hospital room with me, my grandmother had them to exit. After they left, my grandmother asked me a question, and after I responded, she laid her hands on me and said ever so calmly, "don't worry, you are going to be alright." I stayed in the hospital for three days only to baffle the doctors, the issue I had was gone, no trace of any problems; there were no signs of anything ever being wrong with me, I was released that day. GLORY! There was another time, I saw her lay hands on someone's head, a large knot was visible, but after she laid hands and prayed, the knot was no longer there nor any signs of the knot ever being there. There was no bruising, no scars, nothing. I was clueless as to how anointed she was, and the power that rested upon her life, until I, became more mature in the Lord. I just thought she did what all "grandma's" did and make situations better by their mere presence. When grandma would arrive there were longer any issues, any problems or any confusion. Everything would cease.

It was truly a blessing to have such amazing people in my life to groom me, teach me and to show me what real holiness looks like. I did not understand, why they took such time with me in this manner. I had no idea what I was being groomed for, but, now it has become so clear, it was all for His Glory. These three lovely people showed me a life of holiness is possible, if you want it. I remember my uncle K.C. would say "I love you and there is nothing you can do about it". He would also say, I was his favorite niece but the amazing part about that, he would tell all his nieces the same thing, he had no favorites, just an amazing love for everyone. My uncle Earl, on the other hand was a bit different, he was very straight forward, and he did not play. It was either you are living right, or you are living wrong and going to hell, period. I use to think he was so rough around the edges, as it turns out, I, too am very no nonsense(rough) when it comes to God.

My grandmother set the bar so high for Christian women, so it is extremely difficult for me to understand, women in the church today especially older women; the misconduct, the meanness, the rudeness, the gossip and yet profess to be Women of God, see my grandmother did not display any of those attributes. One of her greatest qualities, she did not judge, no matter how many mistakes you made. And believe me, I made plenty. She never made me feel condemned in my mistakes. She would tell me, "make sure you keep your skirt tail down." I would respond, "But grandma what if I ain't wearing a skirt?" She would giggle but, I knew exactly what she meant. I also knew she was not playing. I never saw my grandmother angry (I'm not saying she didn't get angry, I never saw it), I never heard her use profanity, I never heard her gossip or act any other way except Godly. My grandmother is a tough act to follow. "They don't make them like her anymore."

All three of their approaches were different, but it was all God, and it allowed me to have such a well rounded out look on God, what a real relationship with God looks like, how we are to act as Christians and the love we should show as Christians. It is difficult for me to understand anything less than what I have been privy to in my life. Holiness, and Love. I had three great examples....so now, when people encounter me, they will have a better understanding to why, I become so vexed in my spirit, when I see foolishness in the church, why I am no nonsense when it comes to God and why I cannot and will not accept any excuses for not living holy; I have seen holiness modeled, I have seen what righteousness before the Lord looks like and I have seen through these three what the Love of God should be like. They lived a life to please God without wavering and due to their example, I, too, will live to please God.

CHAPTER ONE

Church Hurt

Church hurt is one of the worst hurts a person could experience, and it is one of the most difficult hurts to overcome. I believe the pain is so debilitating for some as it is an unexpected hurt. You believe you are walking into a church, a place of refuge, a place of peace and a place where you will experience God. Only to experience, anything other, than God. You have no idea you should walk in church with your guard up, but, why should you, it's church. You think every pastor is anointed and loving because they are pastors and you may think every church members is godly because they are in church. So, basically, you have nothing to fear. As I thought. This is church, and these are church people so why would I, fear? They are quoting scriptures, their dressed modestly, their speaking in tongues, their preaching, their prophesying and praying so *what would I have to fear*?   The more I experienced, the more, I recited, "These are church people, I do not have anything to fear." I began understanding this scripture, Matthew 7:15, "Beware of false prophets, which come to you in sheep's clothing, but inwardly are raving wolves."

The hurt, I experienced included so much disappointment, extreme sadness and great astonishment. To witness people claiming to profess Jesus Christ as their Lord and Savior, claiming to know Him and claiming to have a relationship with Him but conducting themselves in ways, that are against everything He stands for. Very disheartening. The primary people who are inflicting such hurt in church are those who know scripture, attend service every Sunday, have positions, and operate in gifts.

Another reason I believe this hurt is so debilitating, those who caused hurt shows no remorse as they continue to freely function in churches, service after service, meanwhile, moving from person to person, hurting and destroying people in the church at their leisure.

When I think nothing else could shock me, then there is always something else that shocks me. There was a lady who gave me a word and said, it is from God, but I overheard her speaking negatively about me just moments earlier. How could this be? Would God operate this way? Is this God? God led me to the scripture in Romans 11:29, "For God's gifts and his call are irrevocable." This scripture comforted me, it did not lessen the pain but it made sense.

God began revealing so much more, I began to see people operating in gifts without God, delivering messages not of God and yet saying, God said. As my spiritual eyes were becoming more in tune to the spirit of God, I could now see spirits operating in people, the motives and the ill intentions of people. There is a thin line between a word from the Lord, and a word people say is from the Lord. 2 Corinthians 13:5, "Examine yourselves to see whether you are in the faith; test yourselves. Do you not realize that Christ

Jesus is in you-unless, of course, you fail the test?" Many in the church are failing test due to the lack of self-examining. As I continue to mature in the Lord, the more aware, I became of what is and is not God. I rebuked myself for many years, I, honestly, did not want to believe people were this bold in their deception in the house of God. I was so naïve, so gullible in believing all church people were good. This was a hard pill to swallow especially from my upbringing, I had to realize there are real life demons in church and they are there every Sunday in positions.

After attending a service, a young man asked me, "Why do you continue attending a church when every time you leave, you're crying?" I thought to myself, I had to stay here, the words were spoken, if I left, my life would fall apart. I honestly could not answer him so I remained silent. He states," When I get older, I'm never going to church, if this is how church people treat people and why do they say all those mean things to you". My response to him, "I think, I have done so much wrong to God, this is my punishment." I attended another service, at the same church, as I was walking to my car, crying, once again, a lady pulled alongside me and said, "What they're doing to you in there, is not of God! There is no reason, for you to walk out of church worse than what you were before you went in. God is not pleased and He will deal with them." At that moment, I thanked God. I knew I did not deserve it but then again, I thought, I did, because it was happening in the church, no one in the church was disputing it so I thought I deserved it. I honestly, thought something was wrong with me and I was beyond repair. Wait a minute, these church people would not lie on God, would they? Not these people. Not these church people who has been in church for a thousand years, they would not allow the devil to use in church at my expense. This cannot be so. Right? BUT IT WAS, IT WAS NEVER GOD. Why should I have ever to question any of this, I was in church, and these were good Christian people, right? Church hurt has cause people to turn away from the church and turn away from God. This hurt in church and with church people is unfathomable. On numerous occasions, people have expressed; they would rather take their chances with people in the world because they know what they are getting but with people in the church, you are not aware of what you are getting until it is too late.

My prayer: Lord God, I pray right now for every person who has experienced hurt and is experiencing hurt right now, heal them, allow them to understand these things sent out against them, were intended to prevent them from rising to their rightful place in You. By the power of the Holy Ghost, they shall rise and be all You have anointed them to be in Jesus Name, Amen. Do not allow tactics of the enemy prevent you from progressing in God. The enemy uses people/church people to try and destroy God's anointed, but God's plan will be made manifest in your life. Do not allow any circumstance, any situation, any person hinder you. GOD CALLED YOU!

Although, I was hurt in church, I could not continue in a place of hurt. I had to come out of that place for you and for me. I had to ensure the plots and plans of the enemy are revealed. I had to confirm for you, yes, hurt exist in the church but you are better for it now. My going through was not in vain, I learned great lessons in the midst of it all. I learned, I had to know God for myself, not what I heard of Him but I had to develop an intimate relationship with Him. My experiences taught me more than I ever thought I needed to know. THROUGH THE HURT I LEARNED WHO I AM TO GOD AND HOW EFFIECTIVE AM FOR THE KINGDOM OF GOD. The events that took place in my life were painful; I pray through my vulnerability and transparency someone will become strengthened, know without a shadow of a doubt God has confidence in you and that you will make it through. God does hear you, and He sees all of what you are going through. He is fighting every battle for you, and you will come out BETTER. I promise. Look at me, the one who endured so much hurt in church is being used for such a time as this. For each person going through right now, there is someone waiting for you to come out so they can become strengthen by your testimony, someone is waiting to be encouraged by your trials, someone is waiting on your victory so they too can see; if God did it for you then He will do it for them as well. I had to remind myself of this with each blow the enemy hit me with; I will not allow the hurt to consume me because someone is awaiting my testimony. I learned a two-fold lesson while I was going through, I am not crazy and, I am who God say I am. No matter how people have tried to discount me, I believe GOD and what He has said about my life; there is

5

more to me than what people thought, there is more to me than what people saw and there is more to me than what people has said. God said, "Before I formed you I knew you(Jer.1:5)."

These events, I am attesting to about church people or in church, is not to discredit God in any way, but to shed light on hurt in the church. The enemy did not intend on me coming out nor did my enemies intend on me helping others from my hurt and pain. If the enemy could have had his way, I would have curled up, gave up or possibly killed myself and killing the gifts and the destiny God placed in me. But guess what; not this girl. DEVIL, YOU LOSE!

Through all of the hurt, I know my purpose, I am here to encourage people, uplift people and show unconditional love, I am here to help the broken and the overlooked, I am here to minister the word of God. I am here to represent God in all that I do. I am here to allow God to use me and my life. Through the hurt from church, I found God, and I found my place in God. The bible says Jeremiah 29:13, "You will seek me and find me when you seek me with all of your heart". I was seeking him and I FOUND HIM Y'ALL! I made a promise to God and myself; I will not stand in judgment of anyone, I will not give the word out of my flesh, I will not condemn others, I will not gather in crowds or plot and plan against others. I WILL NEVER BE LIKE WHAT CAME AGAINST ME.

I love God even more; God, trusted I would overcome every obstacle, I would be untarnished and I would remain faithful to

Him. I am so thankful to the Lord for seeing in me; what I did not see in myself; the strength, I did not know I possessed. Thank you, Lord, for looking beyond my faults, using me and my life for Your Kingdom. When I reflect on all, I have been through, I usually become lost for word but a joy comes upon me, wow; I made it through in my right mind. I made it through stronger, wiser, better and most importantly, I made it through knowing without a doubt, I belong to God. Through my test and trials, I developed a profound love for the Lord, a love the world didn't give me, and the world can't take away. It does not matter what or who comes against me. I am going all the way with God. I got my second wind. I did not allow bitterness to set in, I did not allow anger to over shadow me, I did not let disappointment engulf me. I just became more confident and more determined to live for God and to fulfill my God given purpose. As God has brought comfort to me, I want to bring comfort to you: I BELIEVE YOU! I believe you when you say they hurt you in the church, I believe you when you say they have judged you in church, talked about you and mistreated you, and most importantly I believe you when you say WHO has hurt you. From this day forward know, you are not alone. This may have happened in the church, please do not allow it to turn you from God, please do not doubt who you are to God and how much you mean to God. Please allow God to heal the areas of brokenness and hurt. Allow His healing rain to wash every hurt and pain away so you can be made whole, then use whatever platform God has given you to minister the hope of God, build up others and show the love of God, and be to others what you needed in the church. Love people through the process without judgment, slander, and hypocrisy.

Experiencing, all I experienced helped me to differentiate between church goers and Christians. This pain caused my eyes (spiritual and natural) to become wide open. I am no now more aware of my surroundings i.e. who is standing next to me, who is laying hands on me, the spirit in which they are operating under and I am ever so mindful who speaks a word in my life. I learned to discern (hugs, handshakes, things handed to me, etc.). Transference. The enemy will try to slide one past you if you are not aware. I did not know these things early on, but I got it now through it all, I got it now. The unfortunate reality is not everyone in church is a Christian. There are some Judas' who will eat at your table. Discern and use spiritual insight.

We all are allotted the same opportunity to do the right thing and serve God. People will continue in sin no matter the warnings or consequences; it is a choice. Sin has become so comfortable for some so they will remain in sin. There are people who think their sin is covered up due to church attendance, the ability to quote scripture, but, these are the extremely dangerous ones because they have a form of godliness. But people of God do not be in despair, God has allowed true prophets to see the past the façade and expose sin.

My prayer: Father God, those who are causing hurt in the churches and who are causing people turn away from God and turn away from the church, may these people turn from their wicked ways in Jesus Name. The very poison they are spewing is destroyed by the fire of the Holy Ghost. Lord, locate each person who has turned away from You and turned away from the church and help them to find their way back to You and allow them to encounter real people of God who will love them and nurture and lead them in the right way. I, ask in Jesus name bring forth churches with people who have a real love for You and for Your people. Bring forth people who will not compromise the Word of God. I pray real pastors will spring up and real people of God will begin to rise in You. Father God, convict the hearts of those who are inflicting hurt on the people and cause them to repent, turn from their wicked ways and from this day forward, teach them to show the love of God and be the man/woman of God, you purposed them to be in Jesus Name, Amen.

Just take a few moments and spend with God. BE REAL!

Cry out to God; if you know you are the cause of someone leaving the church, or you have hurt people, gossip about people, judged people or misrepresented God. CRY OUT NOW. He will hear you. Ask the Lord to deliver you right now. Do not allow another moment to pass knowing the hurt you have caused someone. At this moment, GET IT RIGHT WITH GOD. It is no coincidence you are reading this book.

TAKE THIS MOMENT FOR YOU. YOU CAN BE CHANGED FROM THIS DAY FORWARD.

9

Remember this, "For we must all appear before the judgment seat of Christ; that every one may receive the things done in this body, according to that he hath done, whether good or bad (2Cor. 5:10, KJV)". From today forward let it be good that He will see in you.

I want to appeal to those who are experiencing church hurt right now. Today is the day of your new beginning, today is the day of your breakthrough, you are coming forth. You will no longer live in despair, in hurt or inner turmoil as this is your day, this is your day of RELEASE. You will no longer be bound by people, words or actions. I PROPHESY, YOU ARE FREE!

CHAPTER TWO

THE ACCOUNTS-EXPERIENCES

This is one of my very first experiences, it hurt me deeply but helped me in so many ways. I was attending this church not a super large congregation but a nice size. There were people who had been members from the start of the ministry, while others like myself were new. The pastor was very personable and laid back. His wife appeared sweet. She developed small groups for women to establish a sisterhood away from church. I attended a couple of the groups; I was single at this time.

During the groups, women were able to discuss hurts, disappointments, abuse and other issues women faced. I hardly shared, I just listened. What happened next was devastating. The pastor's wife and I had developed a rapport, so when I received the phone call from her to meet for dinner. I was excited. However, this dinner, turned out to be anything but exciting. As we are making small talk. She says, "Let me tell you why I really wanted to have dinner with you". At this point, I began feeling bit sick to my stomach; her tone changed and her attitude. I had to brace myself for what is to come next. She said, "The clothes you wear to church is going to send men to hell. You are too top heavy, so you need to be mindful of what you wear and furthermore to the married men you speak to. Married women have to be careful of single women in their men faces." I had to catch my breath as well as my hands. It took every bit of Jesus to keep me from leaping across the table and laying hands on her and not in the name of Jesus. I was mortified! My response was real bit distasteful, but this literally caught me off guard. I responded by saying, "First, let me say this, I do not want your raggedy husband or anybody else's raggedy husband in the church. But if the men were in church for what I was in church for surely they would not end up in hell. I am confused because your assistant had on something revealing this past Sunday but that does not matter because she is married but, because I am attractive and single, the marry women in the church are threatened. Shameful." Clearly, the dinner was over. After, I left I called a young lady(married) in whom I had become close friends with to tell her of this account, only to hear her say, she was told by the pastor's wife not talk to me because I was single. The young lady and I remained friends. Tax season had approached and I had not received my receipt for contributions to the church so I had to call the church. When I called, the pastor answered, his secretary was out of the office, on this particular day. He was happy to hear from me but, had no idea why I was no longer attending the church. He asked, why did I stop coming. I told him to ask his wife, we ended the conversation only to receive a phone call a few minutes later from the pastor requesting a meeting. I agreed.

I arrived to the meeting, the pastor greeted me as he normal did but, his wife remained seated however she did greet me with a dry hello. As the pastor started the meeting, he prayed. He said, he noticed I had not been in attendance at church. I did not respond initially, I waited for his wife to explain, she did not so I explained the encounter. After I explained, she turned to me and said, "If" I hurt you, I'm sorry". My response was, "No, it isn't if you hurt me, you did hurt me actually you devastated me, I wasn't expecting it from you nor did I understand why this being implied except the married women in the church are insecure as you are; if not you would have approached this differently". I further explained, I wanted to be wrong about what she meant at dinner however it was later confirmed. I was not wrong and it was exactly what she meant. She told, a young lady to end her friendship with me due to me being single. I feel her apology is not heartfelt and her intensions are clear. The look of disappointment on his face. As the meeting came to a close, the pastor said, the sincerest apology on behalf of his wife and any mistreatment, I suffered while attending the church. He repeated several times he really hates to see me leave but he understood. He knew, she knew, and I knew this was wrong on every level and we all knew I was never going back.

ANOTHER ACCOUNT:

Another service at a different church and this actually happened in 2012, one Watch Service, I was on the altar PRAYING to God and someone kicked me. YES, KICKED ME! I could not believe it either, my heart literally shattered into a thousand pieces. Lord, what is wrong with me that someone would kick me, kick me in church and kick me on the altar. I do not believe I had ever cried so hard. Once again, rebuking myself. This time, I needed to know. I wholeheartedly wanted to be wrong. I convinced myself I was mistaken; I kept replaying my position on the altar, the music, the sound of the kick and the physical pain of it. The following day, I contacted someone from the church who actually talked to the church gossip. Every church has one; the one person who knows everything about everyone's business even on days they do not attend church. That one. The conversation went like this: "Do you know what happened last night on the altar, did someone get kicked? Girl, I don't want to get into that. What is there to get into? I just don't want my name in anything." I had the lady end the conversation because If nothing happened then, it would have been nothing to get into. I actually wanted to hear something like, what happened, no, I didn't hear anything like that but instead, girl, I don't want to get into it. I am deeply hurt. I know if the church gossip knew the leader knew or others knew, it was safe to say, it was time to go. I left two and half months later.

ANOTHER ACCOUNT:

I was approached sexually by one of the elder's in the church, I hugged him, and he groped me. He told me, he had been watching me for years and he wanted someone to chill with away from his wife. I acted as if I had no idea what chill with meant so he would stop talking to me. The actions of this man was deplorable but what follow this event had me in total disbelief. I called my leader, I was in tears, as I explained what had taken place. I was told I was not the only; he had done this before. That is not the good part, what happens next is. We had church service the following evening and would you believe who was called to pray the altar prayer. Yes, the sexually inappropriate elder. If this is not the biggest sign, I meant nothing to this ministry or the leader. It is clear longevity with a ministry means everything. I was grossly violated and yet this man was called to pray over people.

ANOTHER ACCOUNT:

I attended a church event, a small setting, they began having Questions and Answers (Q & A). During the Q&A, I made a statement about going back and ministering to the people who I partied with, drank with, the people who seen me out of the will of God. The women in this event began responding all at one time, one said, I was not equipped to do that; one said, it was not my place to do this; one said, I wear wigs and heels, I better be careful I do not end up like the Sons of Sceva (Acts 19:14-16); one said, I was over stepping my authority. I sat perplexed, is this really happening? Are these women really saying these things to me? Yes, they were and no one was found out of order. I actually said it so they would go and reach back to those in whom they smoked crack with, partied with but only to hear them say, they would not ever go back. Sadly, I had been evangelizing for years. Who knew? *disclaimer: it was not my first encounter these women.

ANOTHER ACCOUNT:

I attended another church event, and during this event, a lady I never knew had a calling/prophetic was now up, laying hands and prophesy SOMETHING (can't quite say prophesying). This woman walks around the building; telling everyone God is releasing houses, cars, jobs, money, etc., I was unbothered she did not come to me because I had house, car, job and money. She then makes her way to me and says, "God is mad at you for something you did 2 years ago." She calls me to the front and actually pushed me down as if I fell out behind this word. I cried and prayed and prayed and cried, I wanted so badly to react in my flesh but I did not, I just prayed. Now, I am telling God I am tired of being their pond. I am tired of these church people trying to make it as if God hates me.

ANOTHER ACCOUNT:

I attended a revival, a revival I had no intentions of attending, but, I received a call from a woman who said, there is an anointed man of God delivering a great word. I attended but I wore a pair of baggy overalls, no makeup, and slides (I was told I did not have to get dressed up, so I did not). I arrived late to the church. This man, this anointed man of God began speaking about a Coca cola bottle shape; however, the woman who invited me stated, "He was not talking about that before you walked in". We did not think anything about it because the rest of his message was pretty good. As the service was ending, a line was formed; he began laying hands on people and giving them a prophetic word. I was so hesitant about going up to receive a word, I honestly was not in the mood. I was second to the last or maybe the last person to receive a word. It is my turn to receive a word, and this man says, he needed to "administer" to me after service, and what he had to tell me could not be said in front of the people. I immediately thought the worse. I was smoking cigarettes at that time. He told me to call him after service. He said, the word he had is personal and not for everyone to hear. I was thankful for the discretion but, my mind starting racing. What is wrong with me that I could not get a word in front of the people? On my drive home, I was re-playing what he said in my head over and over again, preparing myself for the worse. I was nervous and scared but I finally called. He then said, I needed to come to the pastor's house. At this point, I am gripped by fear. What could be wrong with me that I have to go to the pastor's house? When arrived to the pastor's house; there were five men from the church standing by the door, I opted to stay outside. I forgot to mention; he was a bishop. When he came out, he said, if I did not mind we could go to Denny's so he could "administer" to me. At this point, I am thinking, we can sit under a coconut tree, just tell me, what you have to tell me. We arrive to Denny's, but now, he says, he will tell me while we are still sitting in the car. WHAT IS SAID NEXT, I WAS NEVER PRE-PARED FOR. When he began speaking those initial things were on point and then his voice changed, and he began telling me, I was not being satisfied sexually and he could satisfy me, he was looking for someone to have his baby; his wife was too old, and he wanted it to be me; I was beautiful. He said, when he first laid eyes on me as I walked into the church, he began thinking of what he wanted to do to me. This entire time, I thought, he was going

17

to deliver some horrific news about me, this whole time, I was terrified. This man had me to come over because his flesh is out of order. Once he started he did not stop, he started sharing with me about the conferences the pastors, bishops attend and how there is so much sex at these conferences (homosexual activities, paid sex services). He revealed, he just had sex with his male cousin; his cousin was curious about homosexual activities. He stated, his wife knew of his sexual appetite so she does things for him anally. He indicated, he would be coming back and couple times a month to run revivals with the pastor, and he wanted me to be his woman in this town. I began praying to God, please make a way out of this for me, immediately, my phone rang. I told him, I had an emergency and that I had to take him back. We never made it into Denny's. Mere words could not explain the pain in my heart. I have always respected Men and Women of God so this was hurtful to my core. I contacted my mother and she then contacted appropriate people, it did not matter. They were still going to let him preach the next day at the revival. However, the service was interrupted by a woman who walked into the church with something wrapped in a white towel demanding his general apology be made direct. He continued with his general apology however this woman would not leave until it was known his intentions, his actions and his premeditated motives. He left the service not because of the pastor but because of the woman made sure of it but I always wondered what was in her white towel.

ANOTHER ACCOUNT:

I attended a women's only conference. As I sat, in the back trying so hard not to be noticed. The MC for the event was the pastor. While on the mic, she began saying women who switch their wigs all the time, "Don't know who they are and are unstable". The women in the conference turned and looked at me. I feel sick to my stomach. Lord, I cannot seem to catch a break with these church people. There congregation was small, I had attended a few church services prior to the conference. I knew from attending their church services; no one switched wigs but me. I sat dumbfounded; I reflected on another female preacher who would throw darts like this in the pulpit. I have seen this spirit before. I will not stay for this. I waited for the right opportunity and left, while everyone was making their plates to eat. I called my mother sobbing like a baby. I could not believe what just happened. Let me explain, I was late because my husband had convinced me to attend in the first place, I had changed my mind several times due to things I had encountered in the past. I was reluctant from the beginning but after much convincing, I decided to go. While speaking with my mother, I receive multiple calls in which I did not answer, initially. The caller kept calling so I finally answered, and it was the pastor's armor bearer asking, was everything alright, and she noticed I left. I told her I would see her later and I was headed home. Only to hang up and receive another call, this time it was the pastor, who summoned me to go back to the conference, out of respect, I turned around and went back. When I arrived, the pastor requested I sit with her at the VIP table in front of the conference. Are you kidding me? Tears streamed down my face the entire time, heartbroken once again. But this time, I did not stop going, I continued attending this church for a couple months after this encounter. It is the end of the year, I decided to attend their Watch Service. The Watch Service was a complete fiasco, and it all began at midnight when they played Kool and the Gang on the PA system, people began dancing the nay nay, a lady had an asthma attack, kids were running around, people were jumping and running. The service became out of order, quickly. I left this service but I did not leave the church. I decided to give it one try. It is the first Sunday of the New Year, I invited a young lady to attend service with me. She discerns well and she is very straight forward. During the service, the pastor said, "Cock blocked" in her message and kept repeating it. My guest looked at me and said, I am never coming here again. It was exactly what I was thinking. We left, and I never returned.

ANOTHER ACCOUNT:

One service, my daughter and I received a word although we did not understand it then, it would be years later as we continued going back to this word. The word released: God would tear us apart. During this time, I did not know at this time, people would look upon you and lie on God. This happened in my early stages of church hurt after leaving my family church. So I had no idea, people did this. After our first BIG disagreement, God took us back to this word. I was so naïve to listen but I not only listened, I outstretched my arms and I received the word. I did not know.

Later I questioned, why would God want to tear us apart. We learned a harsh a lesson about receiving negative words spoken in our lives and result of receiving it and what it looks like.

ANOTHER ACCOUNT:

On my way to service, I received a phone call from one of the elders in the church in need of a ride. I obliged. After service, while waiting for her, she walked up to me in front a group of people and said, "You should be ashamed of yourself wearing too little drawers." I was unclear as to what she was referring to, I did have on white linen pants with black underwear, so I was baffled but more than that I was disappointed she tried to embarrass me in front of others? Why did she not say this when I picked her up for church? Why was she being rude? She stated, she was given permission by the pastor to tell me. Unbelievable.

ANOTHER ACCOUNT:

I had been attending this church and was a faithful tither, I had suffered a broken ankle and was bound to a wheelchair for a period time yet I continued attending church. I pressed my way every Sunday. I never received a phone call from anyone (pastor or members). What I did hear, I suffered the break because I was doing something wrong. I broke my ankle trying to get an oil change early one Sunday morning so I would not miss church. I would sit in back of the church in my wheelchair, I was never asked if I needed prayer not once. I literally had to beg for prayer only to be told prayer on Sundays are for visitors, but wait there are other members receiving prayer. Unbelievable. Even while in my wheelchair, God was dealing with me regarding people mis-using authority and positions. God said, He denied no one prayer. I learned quickly, if people do not like you; they will not want you to be bless, prayer, anything. A lot was revealed to me in that season regarding how people misuse positions/authority out of flesh. I NEVER RECEIVED PRAYER

ANOTHER ACCOUNT:

Right before, I lost my home, I received a check for 2,600.00, and called the pastor, I eagerly wanted to sow half of my check. When I called, the pastor was unable to speak to me but I was given a message, to come. When I arrived, I was greeted very nas-tily by an elder of the church, who said she would take the enve-lope and deliver it. As I am standing there, I see the pastor walk by. I was then told the pastor was too busy to speak to me. At that moment, I felt like taking my seed back but, I began rebuking my-self-saying the devil is trying to make me miss my blessing. I never received a call acknowledging the seed was received nor an-ytime thereafter.

ANOTHER ACCOUNT:

After I was married, a prophet told me, God said, she was to be a prophet to my husband and I. I would begin to get prophecies and calls to have prayer. The one question, I was actually waiting to be asked was finally asked. Can I borrow money? Yes, we loan the money. The prayers and prophecies continued until it was time to pay the money back, the calls became less and less to not at all. Yes, we got our money back. So either she was a prophet to us or not? Why did the prayers/prophecies stop?

THIS ACCOUNT EFFECTED ME:

This is account is about a young man I know, who was faithful in his tithing, would give large amounts of money to the church and would assist the church in whatever manner was needed. However, this man did not know God fully. I saw receipts of tithes paid(thousands) but yet he had no real relationship with God. The people around him was failing him because no one was telling him the truth. He and other members of the church, he attended; participated in smoking marijuana and drinking together. He partied, he fornicated, he continued doing the same thing year after year. According to the people he was bless. Somewhere he was misinformed and misled. He was not being told prophesies from GOD, comes with conditions nor was he told the devil can try duplicate the Word of God to make you think, you are in good standing with God when you are not. When I encountered this young man, my heart pained for him, he had no clue he was hell bound, he had religion (attending church) and his relationship was distorted. He did not think he was bad off because he would receive words of prophesy; he was going to be blessed but nothing about chastisement, nothing about living holy or displeasing God. This misconception and deception went on in his life for years. He did not believe me when I began telling him, the difference between God blessing you and the devil tricking you. He did not believe me because he always had large sums of money in the bank. I would not let up on this young man, I could not and would not allow him to remain in the dark and end up in hell, I needed him to get it. I needed to know I was not against him, I loved his soul to much to allow him to go to hell on a technicality. He often referred to me as the prophet of doom but after many years, he got it, Thank you Lord. God allowed our paths to cross, to save him from a burning hell.

ANOTHER ACCOUNT:

God put me in a position in which I became the confidant to the first lady of a congregation. I had no idea why I acquired such a position. While in this position, I started to noticed this lady sowing discord in the church between the women. She had a controlling spirit. I honestly never felt comfortable being around her but God has me here and I will do what I am purpose to do in this situation. She acted as if people were beneath her, I could never quite understand it because she was not all that however God had me here. God began revealing this lady to me, I could see she had not dealt with her own hurt, disappointments, she was projecting and destroying people because of her pain. One day, I asked why was she sowing discord and I then told her God is not pleased with her actions. What she said next was sad to say the least. She stated, "I cannot have the women joining together, becoming strong because they will soon come against me". I instantly became sick to my stomach. I said/did all that God instructed and I disconnected very quickly.

ANOTHER ACCOUNT:

There was a lady in the church who did not care much for me however around the leaders she would ask me for a hug. She often tried to portray as if I had an issue with her. A couple times, I tried hugging her however on both occasions, my head would hurt instantly. And my rides home would consist of me binding and rebuking every negative thing sent to me from this very contact. After the last episode, I reached out to the leaders to explain, I am at a sensitive time in my life and I need to guard myself so during the time of greeting, I am choosing not to hug anyone. If you could inform the people, it is nothing personal, but I will remain seated as I am going through something. I did not know people would become so offended, even if they did, my request should have been respected. I fail to mention; this congregation was about 15 people; I am more than sure everyone got the memo. As I figured it, there will always be one in the bunch who will try to get laughs or prove they are going to do what they want regardless. Yes, there was one lady who made her way to me and as she was walking toward me she is saying, "I don't care, I'm going to get a hug". I am listening to her say this, I honestly did not want to embarrass her, so I whispered in her ear, "I rebuke this attempt to go against my request in Jesus Name, I plead the blood of Jesus.", I rebuked her subtly but to say the least, I never had those issues ever again. From that experience, I began seeing the boldness of the enemy. I also seen scripture come to life, James 4:7, "Submit yourselves therefore to God. Resist the devil and he will flee from you" I was considered boujee and stuck up, but my authority in God was never questioned and not to mention, no one tried hugging me after that.

ANOTHER ACCOUNT:

My husband and I attended a service where he and I were members at one time. While we were seated, one of the elders got on the mic and acknowledged my husband only. I held a position for many years in this church as my husband did not. My husband looked at me and said, I know we are leaving at offering. How hurtful to be ignored by someone in the church, an elder, who actually prayed with you, laid hands on you. Wow. What did I ever to do her? For the love of God, we were in church. When did the elders get so petty? That is not God.

ANOTHER ACCOUNT:

My husband and I attended a prayer meeting. While in the circle praying, this lady to the left of me, while holding my hand continues stepping on my foot. I moved over to give her room but she continued began praying against this. I finally squeezed my husband's hand so he could see what was happening and he could finally see I say when the demons come after me, is real. He pulled me closer to him. I wondered if he knew what was really happening. I needed for him to see, when I say thing it is real. Ironically, right after we released hands she immediately needed prayer, something started happening to her chest or her breathing so THEY began praying for her.

ANOTHER ACCOUNT:

This encounter was with a group of church women who professed to have been saved, 20 or 30 years yet they gossiped, they were backbiters and even sowers of discord. These women held titles/ positions. The report about these women came from someone who was not seeking God, he pulled me to the side and said, I heard them talking about you. "If this is what Christians do I don't ever want to be one". These people had no idea who was watching, listening and paying attention. This group destroyed a developing friendship between myself and another young lady; the division, gossip, and lies. When I had to have an encounter with these women, I would literally feel sick. One day, I became ill and was rushed to the hospital after collapsing at home, life or death situation. Only to hear from someone else, these women called me a liar, the young lady who told me was actually at the hospital with me. I thank God for witnesses.

ANOTHER ACCOUNT:

I attended a church event and during the service, there were kernels of popcorn being given but in order to get the popcorn, the starting fee was 50.00, for 50.00, you were going to get the big blessing; those who had no money well you might have received one or two kernels not sure if you were going to get the BIG blessing but you would receive a blessing just not as great as those who gave 50.00. I sat and watched this mess of a service. I began looking around to see the expressions of the people; the hurt that was on the faces of those who did not have the 50.00. I sat and wondered, who will believe they are not going to receive their blessing because they did not get the popcorn kernel they purchased at the local Wal-Mart or Publix. Shameful. After the service, I was exiting the building, a young lady was walking out at the same time, who had the look of distress on her face, I asked, "Are you ok?" she stated, "Not really, I wish I had money to get the kernel and the blessing. I had a twofold reaction to this, the humorous side: "You're sad because you didn't get the kernel and the blessing, My God". The spiritual side kicked in, I explained, the blessings of God comes from God not because of the popcorn kernel. God blesses.

Whether you had the 50.00 or not, I told her, remember the widow with the two mites, she gave her all and yet she was blessed (Mark 12:41-44). I started telling her of all the accounts of the bible; I DO NOT EVER remember Jesus having 50.00, 100.00 and 1000.00 dollars to get a blessing. I began explaining further there are times, I gave my last and God blessed me instantly and there have been times, I gave my all and did not receive anything right away but nevertheless God blesses. I told her, I learned to give when the spirit moves me. Tonight, I did not feel led to give to get popcorn kernels. I continued telling her, if you did not have it this time but it is your heart to give, God will make way for you to give. I had to let her know there are times, you may not have it to give because God does not want you to sow in that soil. Sometimes, we just have to thank God whether we have it or not. You may not know why but thank Him anyhow.

ANOTHER ACCOUNT:

There was a lady in church in whom I had great respect but not enough to tell my business but enough that I would help her financially. One day she began telling me her testimony, I felt saddened for all she had gone through. She left it open for me to share. I had always been uncomfortable when people pry and/or ask questions of my life. If I am going to share anything, it will be without pressure, I never felt I ever wanted to share with her. She shocked me as odd being so overly intrigued by my information so I made up a story. I know, I was wrong, I had to, to test my theory. Let me back up, when I say I helped this lady, I helped her on numerous occasions. After I finished speaking with her, I had to write this lie down because if I ever heard it again, I would remember. I never told anyone else this lie. I did not want to have all these weird stories floating around and besides that I knew she could not be trusted. She held a position in the church, and no, that did not make me trust her. I heard her speak of other people business, so I was never telling her anything.

Shortly, after I was married, I heard this story again, so ironic. I knew who told the story; I had only told one such fable. I shocked the person who was telling, I disclosed the name of the person and the story. I explained, I only told this story to see if I would ever hear it again and yet I hear it but only after I am married. I wondered about this, was she trying to hurt me or my husband but at any rate, she failed. And the million- dollar question is, WHY?

*Disclaimer: these events were not in chronological order

CHAPTER THREE

FORGIVING THOSE WHO HAVE HURT YOU

Get a piece of paper. Write down what you experienced, give this hurt to God AND FORGIVE those who hurt you and let it go! Please take as much time as you need to do this, IT MUST BE DONE TODAY!

Have you experienced church hurt? If so, today is the last day that hurt will taunt you, have control over you or hinder you. Today is your day of BREAKTHROUGH, and you will move forth. Right now, you are about rid yourself of the very things that have been holding you back from living your full potential in God. NO LONGER WILL YOUR LIGHT BE DIM, TODAY YOUR LIGHT WILL SHINE BRIGHT IN JESUS NAME.

I want to help you get free today; I want you to be confident God will set you free from everything that has held you back, from every hurt, every negative word, every action formed against you by family, the people in church from the leaders to the ushers. GET FREE NOW!!

I revealed encounter after encounter of what had taken place in my life over the years, while in church and with church people. God had to walk me step by step so I could heal. I did not have anyone to say; I am going to walk with you through this. I had to walk it alone, God and I. As I looked back on it, I would not want it in any other way. God helped me and He will help you also. I want to share how I was able to move past the hurt, disappointment and every other emotion tied to it. Ultimately, it had to start with me. I had to be ready to deal with the truths about myself and where I fell short. Then I had to be real of the people who I respected and the people in position who hurt me. To be honest, I was ready to deal with the truth about myself but for a long time, I did not want to deal with the truth about the people in the church, and the people I had such a high regard. These are people in whom I thought loved me and had my best interest at heart. I had to learn to forgive them those who betrayed me, wronged me and mistreated me. Hanging on to the negative emotions was comforting to me, in that I could justify it. And it made sense to me but it is of God. I had to be ready to get free and not allow hurt to dictate my life any longer. It is easier to speak about the hurt but never fully addressing or releasing it. Holding to hurt validates hurt. After realizing this, I had to be ready to go through the pain of healing. Healing is painful but I was ready to heal. God began walking me through the process. I wrote a lot during this time, writing letters to God and to myself was freeing for me. I wrote, I released and then threw it away. I was not giving it another day of my life. My healing and deliverance became important. And it came. When I knew I was delivered, I could speak of the accounts without tears in my eyes or the hurt in my heart. I then, knew I had forgiven them and I had forgiven me.

Forgiveness, we know familiar scripture Matthew 6:15, "If we don't forgive either will Our Father in heaven forgive us of our wrong doing." I know the scripture, I have read this scripture, and even meditated on this scripture, but now it is time to put the scripture to work in my life. I really have to apply this scripture. But how? How do I forgive those who hurt me without a cause, how do I forgive the frauds, the phonies, liars, the backbiters and how do I forgive those who attacked me? God dealt with me harshly. The question God asked me, "Are any of them worth you losing your place in heaven? If you hold on to the hurt, how does it change them; while it will continue to change you, it will change your heart, it will hinder me from hearing you and lastly, it will separate you from ME eternally." At this moment, I begin asking the Lord, please teach me to forgive my adversaries, teach me how to forgive these people and all others who will come. Teach me to walk in forgiveness. Teach me not to hold grudges. Show me right now how to let it go. If I could be honest, this did not happen overnight. I had to remain constant and consistent to get free. I cried sometimes, I screamed sometimes and I prayed a lot. I had to do it, not for them but for my own soul. I realized if I am waiting for those who wronged me to ask me forgiveness, I would be waiting for Jesus' return.

Forgiveness is not easy, but it is necessary. It is necessary for you not for the other person, it is necessary to help you not to lose your place with God. Unforgiveness will harness your blessings. I carried some of these encounters for a long time; I honestly could not believe these things actually happened to me. One of my biggest questions, why did it happen to me? It was harder for me to grasp, I had gone through so much, and how I was singled out for all these encounters. BUT GOD! I often worried would people actually believe this happened to me and it happened in the church by church people, and by people who carried titles? Who would believe me? I began thinking who in their right mind would want to have all of this information, who would want to make any of this stuff up and who actually would want to take time and write these thing down to help someone else if it WERE NOT TRUE. My purpose of writing these accounts, to let others know you are not alone, I made it through it, and you will to, I also want those who are continuously hurting people to stop before it is too late and repent. I now know, I did not deserve the hurt, the mistreatment or any of those things that happened BUT I AM BETTER FOR IT NOW. Forgiveness was my only "Option."

Today we GETTING are free, and today we will walk in FORGIVENESS; God said. When I minister to others and began sharing, I get praise in my heart. I praise Him because I did not allow any of these situations or circumstance to turn me away from God. I love the Lord with all my heart, with all my mind, and with all my soul and all that is within me. Shame on the devil for trying me.

IT IS TIME TO FORGIVE AND MOVE ON, NOW!

Forgive them so God can be glorified. Take a brief moment before moving forward and scream to the top of your lungs. **I FORGIVE** insert the name/names here_____. **I FORGIVE THEM LORD**

FOR insert the hurt here_____.
(repeat as many times as needed). From this day forward DE-CLARE this hurt will no longer dictate my worship, my praise, my life, my prayers, my blessings and ultimately it will no longer hinder my relationship with My Father. **REPEAT THIS, IT IS OVER!!**

CHAPTER FOUR

WHAT DO YOU DO TO OVERCOME THE HURT?

Now, we have forgiven those, who have hurt us and forgiven ourselves for holding on to it for as long as we had. Now, let us start the process of overcoming the hurt; first, you have to acknowledge the hurt has taken place then make the same declaration to God. Be real of the pain; it is yours. Do not allow anyone or anything to sway this feeling. Often, we excuse our pain because it does not make sense to someone else. Express it. Acknowledge your own feelings of the accounts. If it is a pastor, acknowledge it, no matter if it is a pastor, bishop, the apostle or the first lady, whomever. Do not, I repeat, do not change the accounts to appease someone else. You are better equipped to deal with the truth, leave it there and move on. If you allow people to dictate to you what you are saying has taken place, you will never get free. I want you to get free today. I do not want you to allow another day to go by with this hurt, the disappointment, and betrayal. It is leaving you today in Jesus Name. Acknowledge it, do not suppress it any longer. As Christians, we walk around with the fear of saying this person hurt me, due to their position. Position or not, hurt is hurt. People misuse this scripture, Ps. 105: 15 "Touch not my anointed and do my prophets no harm." The misuse of the scripture makes people afraid to say this pastor hurt me or this bishop or apostle. I have seen people stop in midsentence out of fear to share their hurt. Speaking of your hurt and speaking negatively are two totally different things. People are walking around here spook to tell the truth about how mistreated they have been and are being. Is it ok for the pastor to speak negatively about his/her members? This often confuses me. It took me a while to get pass all the mumbo jumbo and say, "I have been hurt." I had to say this out loud to myself so I could process the hurt. We often think masking it, covering it up will somehow make it go away. Never addressing the hurt, is such a disservice to you and your spirit. Unresolved hurt will eat away at you and will hinder your growth in God and imprison you to this feeling of hurt. The unresolved hurt is now blocking your praise and worship and is preventing you from tapping into the spirit of God like you did before you experienced the hurt. So in actuality, you are losing. You are losing that intimate place in God. You are overwhelmed by the hurt, and it is consuming you. You are taking so many losses, but the person who hurt you is unbothered. When processing and releasing the hurt gets unbearable: Remember Our Lord and Savior and the pain (hurt) He suffered. John 10:10, "I come that they may have life, and that they might have it more abundantly." We must endure it for Him. When we ask God, give us more of you, but we have no clue what that consists of. And wanting more of God is not a bad thing at all, it just comes with a price but in order to get there, you have to OVERCOME THE HURT!

CHAPTER FIVE

THE CROWD vz. STANDING ALONE

I did not know, I had to stand alone. In this process, it was no one but myself and God. In standing alone, I would not give in because groups or clicks. I often found most church people ran in clicks, and these clicks; I wanted nothing to do with. Through the trials, God was teaching me to stand alone, stand alone in his truth and stand alone in him. I was never alone even though the crowds against me were great in numbers. I was often reminded of Hebrews 13:5, Be strong and of a good courage, fear not, nor be afraid of them: for the LORD thy God, he *it is* that doth go with thee; he will not fail thee, nor forsake thee". I asked God, why are there always many who would come against me and, He spoke and said, *"People never came against Me alone, there was always multitude who banned together against Me, so why would you think it would be any different for you". I said to God, but I am one person and they are many. God said, "He who rested on the inside of me is the same who rests on the inside of you. As I stood, you will too stand. They misunderstand you because they first misunderstood Me". As I am talking to God, I said Lord; they draw alliances against me. When God spoke this, "He said, most people cannot stand on their own, so they need crowds. Had they sent only one in the Garden of Gethsemane, he would not have overtaken me; he actually would have been changed, so they sent in an army to physically subdue me as they do to you. They come against you in numbers to intimidate you but even then it does not work as it did not work with me, I had a purpose and so do you. God said, do not fear the crowds; in the crowds you can clearly see who is for you and who is against. Watch the faces of the people, see the spirits of the people, discern in the crowds. In the crowds, many will be saved, many will hear My Word; in the crowds, many will turn from their wicked ways; in the crowd is where the woman with the issue of blood was made whole. There is a two-fold dynamic to the crowd, but in the crowd, I am always present".*

As I reflected on the crowds and how I stood alone, it was heartbreaking but yet inspiring. How can a person be hurt and happy at the same time? For so many years, I experienced people being cool with me and then out of nowhere they were not, like from hot to cold instantly. For so long, I remained baffled. He reminded me, I asked to be delivered me from people and not allow me to be a crowd seeker or a crowd pleaser. I experienced losses of friends, people who I held dear to me. For a period of my life, I knew people were around for what I could do for them. I remember in middle school, a girl said to me, she became friends with me only because everyone knew on Friday's I went to buy pizzas for whoever was with me. I remained puzzled for many years, the process had already begun and I did not know. I was being prepared for who I would become. I have come to terms with it all. I count it as a blessing to have those God said they could be here. I, now, ask if this is seasonal or lifelong, or is it for me to assist them or for them to assist me. This helps me to deal with everyone who enters my life accordingly. So whether people are around or not, I have learned to be abased and abound (Phil.4:12, KJV).

Standing alone was a challenge, as humans, we have this innate desire to be wanted and needed. And it is not that I am so deep that I do not have feelings, I have just learned to watch the crowds. I have seen prophets stumble over giving an authentic word of God to a friend. Standing for the truth is ultimate, standing for the truth no matter what. I needed this process of standing alone, I never want to compromise my position with God for people's acceptance.

God began revealing many different things through dreams, visions and in my time of meditation about people. There are people in positions in churches who did not have the spirit of God, every other spirit than God. Revelation after revelation, people I had encountered and those I would encounter. I started smelling certain things, and he (God) would let me know what these smells were and why certain smells were present. I remember going this service, and I stood next to a young lady (minister), and this smell was horrific, this smell made me a bit nauseous, this is what uncleanliness smells like not just fornication this is the stench of unrepentant sins; God said, "These are the stenches that come before my nostrils. The reason she remains in sin and in position is because she is part of the crowd".

As God is dealing with me regarding crowds, I was able to go and attend different churches, prayer groups, and prayer calls and there was always a word released unto me: God is placing a boldness in me to be used for correction with leaders (apostles, bishops, pastors. Etc.). Words released: People do not want to receive the word the Lord places in you but speak it how God gives, and He will prove His word, do not add to it or take away from it.

God place this no non-sense attitude in me regarding His Word. I will not be swayed by the crowds. This is not for a popularity contest with man but as long as I am obedient to the Spirit of the Living God, it is well with me. As God made sense of my seasons. God will make sense of your season even if you are standing alone.

During this time of standing alone, I attended this church, and as I sat, I saw the sword of judgment on the altar. So, of course, I immediately started to rebuke myself. This cannot be, as I saw the sword, God began to take me through the church, and all these other things were being revealed. There was great division in the church as well as confusion, and it all originated from the leaders. The wife was holding resentment in her heart for many things which had taken place in her marriage. Instead of building marriages up, she began tearing them apart; condoning separation and divorces. Due to the pain the husband caused in the marriage, he allowed it to take place without correction. I wanted to know why these people in the church is sitting under this. They are a part of the crowd. When you open the door to sin,

41

here comes sin and his homies to take over the place. The church was having a hostile takeover by sin; no one cared because they with the crowd.

Every day, I have a choice to stand with the crowd or stand alone, if it means I have to compromise my relationship with God, my place in heaven or my position with God, I choose to stand alone.

CHAPTER SIX

WOULD YOU BELIEVE THESE THINGS ACTUALLY HAPPENED IN THE CHURCH?

I had no idea such hurt would happen in the church or that it would happen to me however it did, and it had happened for a long time. I never knew, I would ever be in a position to let others know of these things in the church. God used my character, people who know me, know, if it did not come from God, I will not speak it. I am so bold with telling the truth to whomever. Who will believe these things are happening in the church? People will believe. These thing will be uncovered. These things can no longer continue in the House of Worship or in the House of Prayer. People are being hurt and turning away from God, and it is grieving God. People who have caused any to fall shall surely suffer. God sent, people in specific buildings to receive love, shelter, salvation, and many were turned away and ended up using more drugs, drinking more, hurting more, and people formed clicks alliances in the churches, and yet rejected those God sent. The blood is on their hands.

Even as I start writing, God told me to write what I am telling you to write, "*I (He) will prove every word of it, so do not concern yourself with people who try and discount you, do not worry when people say this did not really happen. Out of your obedience, the truth shall be revealed. Do not try and defend yourself;*

the truth needs no defense, and those who will try can come against thee with negative words, I, the Lord thy God, will defend thee. You are no longer to be silenced, and I will continue using you; you bring Glory to my name. People can no longer pretend as if they are oblivious to how they have hurt people or you. People have been hurt while seeking Me, people are continuously being hurt seeking Me but remember My Word, Duet. 32:35, "It is mine to avenge, I will repay. In due time their foot will slip, the day of disaster is near and their doom rushes upon them."

This book is out of obedience to God and in my obedience to Him, I must speak of things I may not personally want to speak on, but I will take being obedient to God- for one hundred, Alex. This is concerning the leaders, there are times when leaders confuse pastoring and control. I am unsure if control comes in due to greed for money, power or self(flesh). God does not make anyone serve Him, these are choices so then how can a man or woman make person/people do the things you want them to do. This is where I believe the enemy gains access. Control is a spirit, and it is not of God. An open door is an open door. The spirit of control enters in and other sins creep in but are overlooked; like the deacon being so entangled with sexual demons, but teaching bible study or the minister in which man appointed is fornicating and laying hands on people, or active homosexuals is preaching in the pulpit because they can draw a crowd. Control is granted access from the head. Now everything is out of whack.

The entry way or the access in the church are the pastors. Pastors; people belong to God. God entrusts, the people unto you so you can guide them, love them, equipped them, teach them, support them, lead them, pray for them NOT TO CONTROL them. Example of control: There was a young lady some many years ago, who prayed on a prayer line faithfully. This young lady enjoyed the line, and while on the line blessings had manifested in her life, she would get the charge she needed. One day, this young lady was told by her pastor if she continued on the prayer line, she could not attend the church. I could not make up something this ridiculous up if I tried. The disturbing part of this is, the young lady stopped getting on the line openly, but would get on secretly and not pray. I am very unclear even to this day to the purpose behind it except it, I know it was NOT of God. This pastor operates under the spirit of Jezebel spirit then and now. I also know of other pastors who will forbid "their" members from fellowshipping with other churches. I believe offering has a lot to do with it.

Some things have taken place in the church that confuses me even to this day; I am still confused. As we know God is not the author of confusion (1 Cor.14:33). This is another ungodly behavior that takes places in the church and with church people and this happened to me. When I think of it and share this, I always find myself shaking my head. The only clarity I have received in regards to this is; is miserable people find ways to bring misery into the lives of others. Besides the spirit of control; Jealousy is a

45

cold beast among church people. The spirit of jealousy is prevalent in the church today and it tries to be portrayed as basic insults or mild gossip.

There are married women who are actually jealous of other married women. There are married women who will actually prey (spelling is correct) against other people's marriages. This is real life stuff, and it happens more often than what people actually think. Some married women will create division in someone else's marriage subtle negative nuggets dropped about their spouses and before you know it the couple is experiencing turbulence in their marriage. I do not understand why women are like this and I clearly have no idea what they would gain from disruption in someone marriages. Why do women, especially church women sit around and speak against someone else's marriage? How can a woman profess to be a Christian speak against another person's marriage, let alone prey against it? Some people do not believe the bible in its entirety, and that scripture applies to us all; everyone, old, young, married, single, pastors, lay man, it applies to all. Galatians 6:7, "Be not deceived, God is not mocked: for whatsoever a man soweth, that he shall also reap". Married women, if you are sowing discord, division, and disunity in marriages, you shall surely reap it. Women be mindful of the things you creep in your marriage by the things you wishing, hoping and spewing in someone else's. When you reap it could or could not happen in your marriage the way you sent it but, it will come back. By way of sickness/disease/ illness, etc. Reflect back on what you have sown. Some women think, if they have been married for a long period, then these things will not find its way back. Foolish. I do not know how you are going to get it back, but what I do know; you WILL get it back. That is the Word of God. God is not going to change His word because of your age, position or the years you have been married or the tongues you speak in. God's word is true, and its good and He will make good on every word.

Hopefully, this will help someone. If you are believing God to answer your prayer and you are reminding God of His Word; He is Jehovah-Jireh, when you need finances, He is Jehovah-Rapha, when you need a healing. So then why would women think, He is anything less than God regarding other people marriages. His Covenant. He will fight for these wives/husbands who are crying out for their marriages and praying about those who interfere.

After my husband and I were married, there were women, married women who spoke against our marriage. I heard things like I married him for money, he married me for sex, but during the time we were married he did not have all of what people thought, he had, and we were not having sex. I also heard a woman whom my husband and I respected say our marriage would not last a year, well, we are at four years. What had I done to her to make her spew such negativity about my marriage? Do women think it is ok to meddle in other people marriages or that it is ok to speak negatively in other people marriages? I have had it done, it is so not cool. I get reports of it daily from others.

This has confused me for a while; my husband received prophesy that he would get married. This prophesy came a few months before we were married. I was not present when he received the prophecy, I was not even in the same state. I had never spoke to him, and he had never spoke to me, but, God made it possible for us to connect and we became husband and wife. What I heard after we were married; was a bit hurtful, to say the least, although he got a prophecy, they did not mean for him to marry me. To this very day, I have no idea why church people are so mean and messy and why do these people who know so little about me, hate me so much? When people do these types of things and say these types of things without cause, what are their motives? My husband paid a lot of tithes his relationship with God was unstable, he helped many people financially yet he was dead spiritually. So was the concern about his spirit or his finances? If they were really of God's Spirit, they would have known, God did this. BUT DID YOU EVER ASK GOD?

Did these women think he was not good enough for me or I was not good enough for him, either way, it was not of God? None of what they said was God, none of how they acted was God, and none of how I was treated was God. Are prophecies only good prophesy if people can control the outcome. Shameful.

To my married couples, I stand praying for you, right now, every negative word sent out against your marriage will be reversed to the sender. Every negative seed, planted in your spouse against you is uprooted by the Power of the Holy Ghost. I speak right now, God shall create a bond within the two of you, no man can break and the wrath of God will overtake those that will try. Lord God, I plead the blood of Jesus over every marriage that has been under attack by jealous people, busybodies and anyone who is being used by the devil. I plead the blood over their marriage, shield and protect the husband and the wife from all hurt, harm, and danger. I speak every Jezebel spirit that is around and about these marriages shall be utterly casted down by the fire of God. I pray every voice trying to encroach these married couples shall be drowned out by YOUR voice. I come against every demonic attack sent out against these marriages; I bind the work and the workers of Satan right now in Jesus name, those that tried to convince the husband/wife to break their covenant is reversed right now. Every seed of discord, disunity, division, divorce, confusion, chaos, negativity and separation is uprooted right now in the Mighty name of Jesus. I speak restoration unto their unions; I speak love to be rekindled within the marriage, I speak in Jesus Name these couple will begin to seek you, together like never before. Lord, teach these couples to learn to keep people out of their marriages and seek You, Lord God for everything. Strengthen every marriage and every spouse in Jesus Precious Name, Amen. Mark 10:9, therefore what God has joined, let no one separate (NIV). Be wise in this hour; the devil uses the people who are closest to you, the people you have respect for, and the people you would not suspect and they are walking in the spirit of jealousy and contention.

THIS TIME TO REFLECT

Reflect back on the problems you have faced in your marriage and WHO responded and WHAT did they say. Did they offer you prayer before advice? Did they offer counsel with you and your spouse? Did they provide you with scripture? Did they provide you with real life situations on how they made it through their trying times in their marriage? Or did they give you ill spoken advice to plant negative seeds in your marriage? Before accepting advice, please evaluate the source. How successful is their marriage? It is a difference in how long a couple has been married and how successful their marriage is. The person you are receiving advice, do they like or respect your spouse? DISCERN! Let us be real, married people, this is on them, but who granted them access into your marriage. The responsibility needs to be placed on the right people or person. How did they get details of your marriage in the first place? You have to be careful who you are letting into your marriage. Know the difference between needing someone to vent to or needing someone to advise you. Know the difference between Godly counsel and ungodly counsel. DISCERN. Just because they are in church does not mean, they have the best advice for your marriage and does not mean they have the mind of Christ, the heart of Christ or even the heart for your situation. Be mindful of who you allow in your marriage, remember the enemy tries to destroy the covenant, so he (the enemy) is not going to use discretion on who he uses. Please be wise to the tactics of the enemy. Some people may not know they are being used to come against your marriage, and then you have others with complete and total knowledge and do not mind being used to come against your marriage. The best thing any married couple can do is KEEP PEOPLE OUT OF YOUR MARITAL PROBLEMS AND SEEK GOD! If God releases you for counseling, obtain counseling from a Christian counselor who loves the Lord and a counselor who has no prior history with you or your spouse.

CHAPTER SEVEN

IS THIS REALLY EVIL I SEE IN THE CHURCH?

I started seeing and hearing things in the church, I could not believe it was real. I often wondered am I crazy, it has to be me, maybe I am not saved, maybe I have the devil in me. How can I actually believe people who have been in church 10-15, 20-30 years are doing these things, saying these things and acting this way. I regularly rebuke myself until one-day God spoke to me and said, "Watch and exactly what you see, is exactly what you see." Lord, I do not want to see any of this or know any of this. These things were strange in the beginning. I would sit in the church, and God would have me to look, watch and observe. The things, I observed were mind blowing and baffling. My very first experi-ence, I remained in a state of total shock for a while. I went to a service, and I saw two ladies speaking to one another, while they were speaking, one turned around and licked her tongue at me. I thought, huh? So I asked God, did I see that in the natural or was that in the spirit. Another account, the same evening, the lady whom she was sitting next to her rolled her eyes at me, and I asked again, is this in the natural or in the spirit. I start praying so hard, binding and rebuking myself, binding the spirit of mental illness, binding and rebuking every spirit sent out against my mind. I began pleading the blood of Jesus over my mind, this could not be real especially in the church. I could not have seen this in this church. God revealed, it was true and these things, I actually saw was real. I began realizing what you see on the surface is not always what is underneath. I thought, I was crazy until other people could attest, this is what they see and have experienced as well. Thank You, Lord.

People try to impress people and to appear a certain way in church but their hearts are far from God. People try to hide behind titles, clothing, etc. and yet God knows them not. Everyone wants to appear so deep in God, but they bear not his spirit. Everyone wants gifts, but they have no heart for the people of God. Everyone wants to be noticed by man and having no idea who Thee Man is.

I was privy to many events that took place in the church, things people thought were hidden God would place me in the right place to see what was transpiring. I could not believe the evil I saw in the church or the evil people I saw in the church. Why do I have to be the one to see the evil in the church. For example, there was a young lady who came in, I had not seen her before however, her dress was a bit short, and her shirt was revealing. She went for prayer, the frowns on the face of the people and they at her something awful. I just assumed those who were staring at her were born saved and never did anything other than live holy, but I know that was not the case, if they did they would have known better. After the young lady received prayer, I noticed her crying, uncontrollably. I checked with her. The cry, she crying was not a breakthrough, cry, that was a cry of hurt, a cry I knew too well. I asked her, if she was ok and her reply hurt my heart, she said, I am never coming back here. My heart became so saddened for her but I saw it all. She was literally treated so poorly by the people who should have embraced her. Shame. After all of that to get a word saying, you need deliverance. My God. This young lady came to church. They did not know her situation; she was in church looking for something but I am sure what she got was not what she was looking for but the evil spirits I saw in them but yet you are standing in judgement of her.

I guess they forgot about the adulterer who prayed over the altar or even the thief who steals from the tithes and offering, but someone comes in looking for something from God only to have encountered the devil. Shameful. Titles and longevity in churches are the passes people receive to get their sins over looked. People are coming in from the street only to encounter these sanctified people; Lord have mercy. The inappropriate whispers and the immature ways in which people from the street are being received is truly a shame before the Lord.

There is evil in the church, and it should not be. How does evil enter into the church? There are points of entry; no one can just come into your house without permission, access has to be granted. The Bible states in Mark 3:27, in fact, "No one can enter a strong man's house without first tying him up. Then he can plunder the strong man's house". I believe this is physically and spiritually. How can someone enter into your house without tying you up; people are so tied up in a mess, the enemy has the opportunity to gain ground and territory in your house, marriage, church, etc. With the (strong man) being tied up the enemy can run amuck.

While God was training, teaching and equipping me, I was able to see so much more than what I wanted to and for a long time, I could not share. I cannot believe it myself so I know no one else would believe. The evil spirits in people, leaving and returning unto people right before my eyes, licking tongues, rolling eyes, turning red, smirks, smell and spirits following people home. There was so much I seen but who would have believed me if I would have said I see evil in the church and with the people who call themselves Christians. Reality is, I have seen evil in the church and no one can ever say ANYTHING DIFFERENT!

CHAPTER EIGHT

ARE THESE REALLY SAINTS OR NAH?

"Not everyone that saith unto me, Lord, Lord shall enter into the kingdom of heaven; but he that doeth the will of my Father which is in heaven (Matthew 7:21KJV)." For so many years, I rebuked myself, of the things I had seen in the church and with church people. I am tired of calling them Christian's because they are not; they are a total misrepresentation of Christ. They are nothing more than church goers, church people or church attendees but surely not Christians. Just because a person attends church for years does not make them a Christian. I had to learn this the hard way, and my perception was crushed. Maybe in the purity of what I thought of God and how I thought people who professed Christ should be, but my cognition was faulty. When I was younger, I thought older people were saved because they are old, Dear Jesus this is so not true. I thought, they are old so the spirit of the Lord was in them. I measured them based on my grandmother being a true Woman of God. But I received the biggest slap in the face. Some of the nastiest evilest women are the elders in the church. The youths expressed; it is the ole' ladies that are the meanest to them in church. A youth said to me; "I won't go back to church because of the old demons that sit in the church on Sundays undetected." I was blown away by this statement. I could not disagree nor comment due to it being my experience as well.

Some of these old ladies are under the radar due to their ages. These are the ones who have learned how to maneuver and manipulate the system. They are the ones who are visible to the pastor and the congregation but are creating so much havoc behind the scene, these are the ones that will appear helpful in public but full of demons in secret. They wait to get people alone and then they can show their true colors. These are the ones who report to the pastor what others are doing so the spotlight does not hit them. These are the ones who hurt my heart because they are supposed to be the examples. This is said in humor but I wonder this: if people are walking around in all this power then why are people blind to the demons of these elders, those who praying over the money, touching communion, and laying hands on people. These people have access to the apostles, bishops, and pastors (the right-hand to man/woman). These are even the people who will head prayer groups. These people will pass judgment on you and feel justified. I met a lady (older) never seen her before in my life and she had so much to say and a great deal of questions, I thought to myself, Lord, does she not see Your spirit in me. And God spoke to me so clear and said, "She does not belong to me". I jokingly thought, I knew my Holy Ghost detector did not go off. How sad is it to be of ripe age and do not know God? What further saddened me with this situation; I can go anywhere, to the grocery store, Wal-Mart, hair salon anywhere and even witches know who I am, and yet this lady is professing to know God and could not recognize His Spirit in me. My God.

People become angry with me, I call it like God shows me and most often than not people will try to make it appear, I do not know what I see or what I am talking about but I go with God and leave the rest to God. I have a boldness God has given me to go and to do His will, and I cannot do it in fear of how people are going to receive me. My forwardness comes from God, talk to Him about it. God graced me to speak to a person/people without judgment but yet tell them the truth. I cannot condemn anyone nor will I, but, I am held to a standard, to tell the truth. What good am I to God if I do not tell you the truth? I cannot be anybody except who God called me to be. People are cool until I began speaking about deliverance and living holy. That is when I get the negative responses. The way I look at it, I will take ANYONE being mad at me than God being angry with me for being disobedient and not telling the truth. These truths are to prevent people from going to hell. I will take my chances with God. Out of my obedience to God, He has given me a platform in which I am expected to bring correction into the lives of the people, some apostles, bishops, pastors. There are many leaders, I have prayed with and for, and have respected the correction, and then there are those who are so in themselves and want to continue in sin, that they become offended, but I do not waver. I do not seek them out; they seek me. For example:

There was an apostle who was incredibly broken, torn actually and he contacted me for prayer, he stated he had been watching and hearing about me, he knew that it was the spirit of God upon me. As I prayed for him, God began to release a word, the reason for the brokenness, he was torn due to him living a double life. He was an active pastor with a congregation, wife, and children and yet secretly participating in homosexual activities.

This man said, and no one, has ever called him on it, as many people (prophets) he has come in contact with and no one has ever told him this "truth." He confirmed it was true. He then told me, he could never speak to me again. I understood he wanted to remain in sin. He did contact again for prayer.

These examples regarding leaders are just as painful for me because I want leaders to get it together. There is a standard for all leaders. Not to be perfect but not to struggle with the same things the congregation is struggling with and surely not in the areas of fornication, adultery, homosexuality, lesbianism, stealing, lying, gossiping, sowing discord or speaking negatively against people or praying against marriages.

My question: Are these really saints or nah? How can you tell the difference?

CHAPTER NINE

JUST BECAUSE WE ARE IN CHURCH DON'T MAKE US CHRISITIANS

There is a certain time in a person's life, when they should want to be sold out to God. There is no more playing or pretending but to have a real relationship with God. The people who are professing Christ does not display his attributes. I have found so many people who may attend church but there is no God, yet they say they are Christians. I often wondered, if God convicts me of the things I do, how can people walk around being rude, mean, gossipers, slanders, busybodies, sowers of discord and every other thing that is not of God and say they are Christians. There was a time in my life, I went to church and continued in sin. I will not make any excuses for it not even now. So when I say these things, I know how the game is played, and I know what double-minded looks like, I know what the religious spirit looks like, I know what playing church looks like, I know what not being delivered looks like, I know what leaving a fantastic service where the power of God fell in the place only to return home to indulge in my pleasures (drinking and cigarettes). If I had to attend service, I would not have sex until after the last service; then I would not attend the next couple of services so no one could actually tell that I was living foul. The most ridiculous thing is anytime I would have sex (fornicate) I would lose large sums of money (thousands), so I would limit my fornication to every six to nine months (boy was I a dummy). I hated when I actually had to, but I had to sustain a relationship.

Which makes the even worse, I knew the guy, I was with was not going to be my husband. While he was around, I did not have to entertain being married. I was driven by business. He proposed, I accepted only to buy time and run my business, but I continued in that mess for five years. But I was sinking deeper and deeper in sin. My business allotted me different perks, invited to VIP in clubs, drinks paid for, and drinks named after my company. This set up is working. The set up was ultimately setting me up. It was my fault; I chose to continue in sin. I was so into self-gratification. I walked around counting the amount of money I wore on daily basis. Oh, you could not tell me anything, I had it going on. I was a business owner and could sit in my pajamas in my home and make money(lots). I could go anywhere in the city, and people knew me from my business, it was great for my ego but yet I was headed to hell.

God has a way of saving your life and you not even know it. I had a major wakeup call, it was the day, I realized I was going to hell and I was taking someone who loves me dearly right along with me. I had lost my business due to being connected with the devil. Before losing my home, one day, I was taking a bath and I was going to end my life by taking a bottle of pills. I did not have the money I use to have. Actually, I had no money, I had no business, and all that I became was tied into things (material things). While in the bathtub, I received a phone call asking me what was

I doing; I said, "I can't take it anymore, I am going to end it". This person immediately hung up and a few seconds later, I hear this big boom, and there was my daughter swinging my bathroom door open, looking at me with tears in her eyes and she said, "I have nobody but you, and if you die, I am right behind you, I will kill myself too." My heart instantly ached. From that moment, I began seeking God for real with my whole heart. It did not take God long to change my mindset and my will to do His Will. I sat in church and was not a Christian, I was a church goer until I wanted God for real. So when I encounter people who are struggling and still struggling with that same thing over and over again, year after year. They do not really want the deliverance. "If you seek Him, you will find him(Jer.29:13)."

People continue in sin because they ABSOLUTELY CHOOSE TO. Continuing in the same behaviors without growth in God is merely a result of lack of relationship with HIM and a lack of commitment to come out of Sin. There are some people who will not stop until they are exposed. There are some who will continue to look the part and attend Sunday services and end up in hell. One of my quotes, "Your relationship with God shows love, the love YOU show, shows your relationship with God."

CHAPTER TEN

I CANNOT STAY THERE

I was unable to stay in certain churches, I could not fellowship and I could not ever return, in some cases, I was perplexed. Now, it is clear, why. When I went to certain places, I had to observe. I visited many churches and learned many lessons along the way, but I could not stay there. In some instances, I felt bad for my husband because he would become so ready to be a part of a church and only to hear me say, I cannot stay there. I cannot and will not remain in a place out of comfortability and familiarity. I have to be free in the spirit, not on guard. Mine and my husband soul means so much more than staying connected to people or places on GP (general purposes). I had to ensure he and I were in the right place and connected to the right people who would minister to us, who would be real in God, where there was real accountability for living holy and the leaders were living holy. We have never looked for a perfect church, we were just needing a place of God, to be surrounded by people who loved God and the people of God really being the people of God. Anything other than that, I could not stay there. I have been through so much; I have become so sensitive to the spirit of God. I ask God about everything and some things I regret I ask because of what He reveals. My connection with people has to be kingdom and I have to protect my husband and I of anything that is not God.

This is the hour when we have to be real in God and find our place in God; if that means praying and fasting until God gives clarity as to where to be planted, hear God. GRAB THIS IN THE SPIRIT. I CANNOT STAY THERE! I cannot stay there; where I am being mistreated, overlooked or talked about, I cannot stay there; when my salvation is of no importance to the leaders. I cannot stay there; where the leaders are out of order. I cannot stay there; when the leaders are creating division, I cannot stay there; when the spirit of Jezebel is running rampant in the church, I cannot stay there; where there is the spirit of greed (money lines), I cannot stay there; when I cannot be who God called me to be, I cannot stay there; where there is hypocrisy. And if I cannot stay there; you should not either.

I cannot and will not stay in a church in which the people are told that elders can curse you, why would I want to be connected to anyone or anything that would ever want to curse me. Why would anyone say, someone else has the power to bring curses in your life? And why would I remain there. I CANNOT STAY THERE! NO SIR NO MA"AM. I cannot stay there; when leaders believe they have the power to "give" another person to someone else. I cannot stay there; when it is ok, for people to use profanity in the pulpit and the congregation not be surprised. I clearly cannot stay there.

I have been privy to many things and that is why I cannot stay there I cannot stay here; when I can walk around the offering plate, and the ministers stink of sex, when active homosexuals can lead praise and worship but the unwed pregnant girl has to sit down from the choir, when the perverted deacon can teach bible study, when the active adulterer can pray over the congregation, when the first lady can sow discord, and it never gets addressed, when the people in positions began speaking curses over someone's life, when people are more interests in money than souls, when church becomes formality, when you have fornicators and adulterers, drunkards on praise and worship team and no one cares, because the music sounds good. I cannot stay there; when the pastor and ministers can spew negativity in the pulpit. I cannot stay there; when the pastor is sleeping with those in the congregation and laying hands on people on Sunday and stating, he does not believe in transference of spirits, I cannot stay there; while pastors are going to conferences and soliciting prostitutes, when the apostle is a closet homosexual and when the female apostle is a lesbian, when leaders try to be so hip they become too worldly, I cannot stay there; when the pastor knows his wife is operating under the spirit of Jezebel but because he has done so much dirt in the past, that he allows her to operate in this manner. I cannot stay there; when there is no accountability to salvation as long as people pay tithes and offering, I cannot stay there; when you get reports of the hurt taken place in the church and it never gets address, when you have a leader who will only believe the first person who tells the story instead of the complete story, when you cannot access your leader because they have become more important than God so you have to go through third parties to access the leader but there is no third party to receive your money, I cannot stay there; when I can go directly to God but not directly to the leader who is here on earth. I cannot stay there; when you share information only to hear it the next service in a propheylie. I cannot stay there; when it is a determent to my soul, I cannot stay there; people do not want God. I cannot stay there; people are too familiar with protocol and nobody is fearing God, I cannot stay there; when leaders are praying against marriages. I cannot stay there; when leaders are speaking witchcraft in the lives of others who they are supposed to be a shepherd over. I cannot stay there; when they will try and choke the very anointing out of me. I cannot stay there; I see the evil, the plots and plans, I see the division, I see the discord, I see the darkness, I see the ungodliness, I see the sword of judgment, I cannot stay there; God is telling me my season has ended, and all I needed to get, I got it so I cannot stay there.

Unfortunately, It is true, leaders will become jealous of the student because of their anointing and their call, but instead of utilizing the gifts within them, the leaders become jealous and starts sowing discord among the members. Believe it or not there are people (leaders) who will try to keep others bound to them and try to drain and diminish their anointing. These leaders are not fully equipped to be a lead and they will always try and discourage you from flowing in your gifts. These types of leaders will never use you to your fullest potential. They will use you sometimes but with conditions. Some leaders believe if they do not ap-point you to a position, then God has not anointed you for your calling. WRONG!! God will use whom HE chooses. Shame on the people in position who are so insecure within themselves, they would actually try to hinder someone becoming who God called them to be. The most powerful thing of it all is NO DEVIL IN HELL CAN STOP God's plan for your life.

It may take some awhile to actually get to the point of realizing you cannot stay there and out loyalty to man can sometimes hin-der your walk with God. Once the chains and scales come off, you will be free to see, if you cannot stay there. PEOPLE OF GOD, please do not remain where God has told you to leave and please do not leave a place where God has told you to stay.

CHAPTER ELEVEN

CAN I GET HELP FROM THE CHURCH?

Can I actually get help from the church? Can I get the assistance I need, when I need help? Who would actually help me? Why do I have to talk to this person and that person when I need help. When there is a need for someone else, I receive phone calls to ask for my help. I remember being pulled out of service on numerous occasion and being asked for money, for birthday gifts, Christmas gifts, donations for this situation or that situation. I always gave without hesitation. I experienced hard times and down to my last twenty-dollar bill. I would go to church with the expectation that God would multiply and most times, He did, but there were times, I would sit in church wondering, if God could tell them He was mad at me and all these other things, did He never tell them, I needed help? So God only speaks mean things about me but never things to help me. I gave to every five and ten offerings that were taken up every service; when I was in need, I was told, to go to God and trust Him. I did learn to call on God. I also learned to rely on God for everything. Even about my giving; many of time, I felt pressured into giving. By not giving me the help I needed. "This was intended to hurt me, but God intended it for my good (Gen. 50:20)."

There are people in the church who gravitate towards people because of money and they will drain you, if you let them. In a valley experience, those people are nowhere to be found. You will hear them later, saying, girl, remember when she had this and remember when she had that but look at her now, she has lost it all. Through tough financial times, common sense kicked in and I learned to stop giving to every sad story I heard; I learned to discern and ask God. If you ever wanted to know how the church or the people in the church really feel about you. Ask for help, and you will see it sooner than later. This is not true for all churches. There are churches who will actually help anyone in need.

There is a fund, I heard of all of my life; I do understand its purpose however my question is why are there, four and five offering and then a benevolent fund? What is the purpose of these funds, when the people who actually donate or contribute to these funds could never get any help? Can someone help me on the benevolent fund and the building fund. I do not know who benevolent is and I never see the building from the building fund. The most confusing part of it is the consistency of taking up these funds but only to ask for special offerings when families are in crisis. Where is benevolent? I know I am being petty but I have always wanted to ask.

I was told no one would help me because I did not look as if I was going through, due to my designer shoes, clothes and handbags. I was so out done to hear this. I cannot get help because I purchased (past tense) nice things, I cannot get help because I am not coming in the church with one shoe on and one show off. I have to look destitute before I can get help. Well I guess, I would not get help; I will not ever look anything short of a King's kid, whether I am going through or not. Sorry, but I am not going to look down trodden just to receive help. God will provide as He has.

This taught me a great deal about perception and deception. I make sure, I consult God on every seed, I release. I encourage each and every one to continue giving and be a cheerful giver. Giving is a gift. Make sure where your giving God is telling you to give and to whom God telling you to give to. Pray for the seed, offering, tithes you release and whatever the intended purpose, it will be used for that. Leave it there, God will take care of the rest.

I implore you, ministries help the people who are in need of help without judgement. Use the funds for the intended purposes. Let people know there is help available to them. There is another side as well. There are people indicating, they are going through situations, only to misuse the help. People of God, discern but do not allow those who are in need suffer because of how the way dress, look or even because of others manipulation of help. Please help people in need, you just never know.

BIRTHING OF MINISTRY

KENNEDY LIN MINISTRIES: I WILL NO LONGER BE SILENCED!

God said, IT IS TIME; I was still extremely hesitant about the ministry. I did not want any added pressure to my life; I only wanted to stay in my lane and live my life quietly. Try telling God what you want to do and He will show you what you must do. God told me, "He can trust me, and IT IS TIME." The confirmation came a few days later on a Saturday morning, I was lying in bed, and I was watching an evangelist on FB, I remembered when she first had started her ministry a few years prior and how much her ministry had grown. My husband seen me watching and said, "Why are you watching other people; IT IS TIME. You can do what she is doing so get up and get started." That morning, I got out of bed and began to put things in motion for the launching of Kennedy Lin Ministries. My husband had no idea, the words he spoke were the same words God spoke to me a few days prior. IT IS TIME.

The birthing process had begun, I had already gone through the labor and the labor pains, now it was birthing time. The birthing of the ministry, it is a highly crucial birth. I needed to ensure the birth was full term not premature and it had all the essential ingredients it needed to grow and as child needs food, vitamins, and nutrients and so does ministry. I had to ensure every nutrient was from God, that this ministry in its infancy would be able to grow and stand and become strong. I did not want this ministry to be as the ministries I had seen in the past. I needed God to be the core of the ministry, I needed humility to be my main ingredient. No matter how big or small it would grow to become the core has to BE GOD. God allowed paying close attention to those who have started small but lost Him along the way. They were humble and when the shift came, they begin to think God needed them instead of them needing God. I wanted to ensure it was not about Kennedy Lin but continuously and ultimately be about God. Initially, I did not ask for any ministry but after I witnessed the hurt, experienced the hurt. I thought God there has to be a better way. I wanted something to help the hurting, the broken, the talked about, and the forgot abouts. I needed to be that person in which people would know you are loved no matter what and where they would receive unconditional love. I had to "go through" for ministry. "To whom much is given, from him much is required (Luke, 12:48, NKJV)."

Kennedy Lin Ministries is a ministry where people can receive what I never received, unconditional love. God has a mandate on my life to show the love of God. The love, I longed for but never received from those with titles, from family members, those I attended church with and even those I worked with who profess Christianity. This type of love God is requiring of me and it goes far beyond just saying I am a Christian. Every one of my trials were not just for me but for ministry. I did not go through to write this book but through my experiences this book was manifested.

Hopefully it will speak to those who have and had felt unloved, mistreated, unappreciated, overlooked, used, abused even for those who needed for someone to acknowledge the hurt they experienced in church and by church people. I pray right now, for each and every person who is experiencing hurt in church, by church people, may the peace of God over take you right now, may the love of God fill your heart right now and every feeling of inadequacy, hurt and disappointment is destroyed by the Power of the Holy Ghost, every plot and plan of the enemy that wanted you to give up on God by sending these imposters in your life to hurt and frustrate your purpose is removed in Jesus Name. Where they thought you were going to through in the towel, your towel is now raised in victory. You are being strengthened right now. The King of Glory is and will fight each and every one of your battles for you, the battles you know of and the battles you know nothing of. You are victorious because God said in Jesus Name. I prophesy right now that everyone who is not for you will be exposed and removed from your life, the backstabbers who smile in your face and spoke curses over your life subtly shall be removed by fire. Every jealous, envious, sower of discord, gossiper, backbiter, liar, slandered will be exposed by the same method they used to hurt you, they will reap everything they sowed. No longer will they throw a rock and hide their hands. Everyone who tried to discredit you and your anointing and position in God shall be put to shame. Every person who provided ungodly counsel which resulted in the demise of your marriage, career, housing or business

Kennedy Lin

shall reap what they sowed, every person who put a business deal together making you to lose everything; I say to you today that God is going to restore everything that was lost (home, money, status, cars) in Jesus name. It is so.

Every dime scammed from you by way of internet with factious businesses, every dime scammed by factious businessmen and women shall be returned to you a hundredfold. For every boss or supervisor who plotted your dismissal under the grounds of jealousy, envy or because of the reason of your anointing which resulted in a loss of finances, home, family, cars, they shall be measured by the same measurement you were measured by. For every time you put your last dollar in the offering or sowed a seed, may God allow you to see your harvest, NOW! Every person's life you have sowed into and for every ministry, you have sowed into and did not receive good measure, press down, shaken together, running over and where men did not give unto your bosom. It shall be given into your bosom NOW, for every time you placed your last in the Man of God and Woman of God's hand and you did not receive your reward but for your obedience, those finances are released NOW. For every person God told to bless you and they held the blessing back, they shall release it now. Every person that uttered negative things about your ministry, you, your husband/wife children, unborn children, your finances, your home, your marriage, your future shall be put to shame right now. God is keeping every promise He has promised you. I speak that every prayer of witchcraft, is reversed right now. The blood

74

of Jesus covers you, your spouse, children, home, work, ministry, your finances. For every person/people who plotted against your ministry/church which resulted in your loss, God will bring back all that was lost in this season.

After reading this prayer, I pray a shift has taken place in your spirit, your atmosphere, your joy, your peace and future. I pray this change is evident in your life and other will see your light has been ignited in Jesus Name. I prophesy your seeds (money and children) will be blessed, YOUR breakthrough shall be released NOW!

Kennedy Lin Ministries had very little to do with me but everything to do with God. God knew placing such responsibility on me, I would do the right thing in honoring Him. I am no longer hurt by the things I have been through, I no longer question, why am I going through this and that. Kennedy Lin Ministries: I WILL NO LONGER BE SILENCED! There has always been purpose for my life, I had no idea but God knew as I am reminded of the word, "I knew you before I formed you in the womb; I set you apart for me before you were born; I appointed you to be a prophet to the nations. (Jer.1:5 ISV)." As you can see, there is a purpose for Kennedy Lin Ministries and for Prophetess Kennedy Lin AND IT HAS BEEN APPROVED BY GOD!

SPECIAL THANKS

YOU PUSHED ME SO THANK YOU

Thank you to all my haters, and my doubters-YOU PUSHED ME!

Thank you to my husband (Andreas Morgan), you are shy of amazing. You are a dream to have in my life, and you have undoubtedly supported me through the good times and the bad, I thank you, so much for all your support, I love you more than you'll ever know, my life is complete as you were the missing pieces to my puzzle, because of you, I CAN, soar with the eagles. Peaches Coleman (My Mother) thank you for your everlasting support and love. You consistently give me the courage to do more and strive more and to never give up on myself. You have taught me to live and to be unapologetic about my life and who I am. A million I love yous or thank yous would never be enough. You are so appreciated. To my daughter "Bella," Neek Neek, my #1 since day one, you have been that thriving force pushing me to do better, be better and ultimately become better, I owe so much to you for your constant push and belief in me. You are a blessing to my life. I love you more than words could ever express. You are too amazing for words.

It is so incredible to have people in your life who actually want to see you succeed and for those I am thankful. Those who have stood praying for me and with me, rooting for me and cheering me on the whole way through with this book, with my life and with my marriage; a great big thank you and God bless to each and every one of you:

Pastor Joseph L. Moore(ALWAYS MY PASTOR), Coach Donna Jean, Prophetess Collette and family, Apostle Barbara Thomas, Apostle Eugene Taper and family, Prophet R.K. James and Lady Christie, Pastor Timothy Shockley, Sr., Prophetess Teri Raven and family, Prophetess Ranelle Grace and family, Evangelist Oladimeji Ayodeji, Prophetess Cindy Vereen, Kelly Gillian, Kimberly Rutherford-Miller, Kato, Nelson Lawton, John Singleton, Monique Pratt, Kira and Jeff Brown, T. Huddleston, Pastor Tymon and Theodisia Moore, Kerisha Brissett, Mary Grace, and to the little ones: Bentley Prince Morgan(puppy) you have brought so much joy to my life, Jazmyne Ramirez, Cali Faith Brown, Eddie Ramirez III, Jordan Ramirez and Calib Brown. A special little boy: Devontate. Thank you to everyone who will support me in obtaining a copy of this book and the other books to follow. Be Bless and know that I love you so much.

~ Prophetess Kennedy Lin~

k.lin.ministries@gmail.com